Oceans of the World

Arctic Ocean

Louise and Richard Spilsbury

raintree
a Capstone company — publishers for children

Raintree is an imprint of Capstone Global Library Limited, a company incorporated in England and Wales having its registered office at 7 Pilgrim Street, London, EC4V 6LB – Registered company number: 6695582

www.raintree.co.uk
myorders@raintree.co.uk

Edited by Penny West
Designed by Steve Mead
Original illustrations © Capstone Global Library Ltd 2015
Picture research by Tracy Cummins
Production by Victoria Fitzgerald
Originated by Capstone Global Library Ltd
Printed and bound in China by Leo Paper Group

ISBN 978 1 406 28754 7
18 17 16 15 14
10 9 8 7 6 5 4 3 2 1

British Library Cataloguing in Publication Data
A full catalogue record for this book is available from the British Library.

Spilsbury, Louise and Richard
Arctic Ocean. – (Oceans of the World)

Acknowledgements
We would like to thank the following for permission to reproduce photographs: Getty Images: Christian Aslund, 23, Kim G. Skytte, 8, Raimund Linke, 16, Timothy Allen, 10; Newscom: EPA/YONHAP, 7 Top; Shutterstock: Andrzej Gibasiewicz, 15, Christopher Wood, 25, Harvepino, 17, Cover Middle, Henri Vandelanotte, Cover Top, Incredible Arctic, 4, La Nau de Fotografia, 24, Michal Piec, Cover Bottom, Natalia Davidovich, 11, Olinchuk, 6, ppl, 21, Rainer Lesniewski, 7 Bottom, Zmiter, 13, Design Element; SuperStock: Exactostock, 18, Jason Pineau/All Canada Photos, 19, Kerstin Langenberger/imagebroker.net, 14, Nordic Photos, 26, Olivier Goujon, 22; Thinkstock: dusko matic, 12; Wikimedia: Algkalv, 27, Ansgar Walk, 20.

We would like to thank Michael Bright for his invaluable help in the preparation of this book.

Every effort has been made to contact copyright holders of material reproduced in this book. Any omissions will be rectified in subsequent printings if notice is given to the publisher.

All the Internet addresses (URLs) given in this book were valid at the time of going to press. However, due to the dynamic nature of the Internet, some addresses may have changed, or sites may have changed or ceased to exist since publication. While the author and publisher regret any inconvenience this may cause readers, no responsibility for any such changes can be accepted by either the author or the publisher.

Contents

Some words are shown in bold, **like this**. You can find out what they mean by looking in the glossary.

About the Arctic Ocean

The Arctic is one of the world's five oceans. The Arctic Ocean is the smallest ocean of them all. An ocean is a huge area of salty water. Altogether the oceans cover two-thirds of the surface of the Earth.

The Arctic Ocean covers the most northern region of Earth.

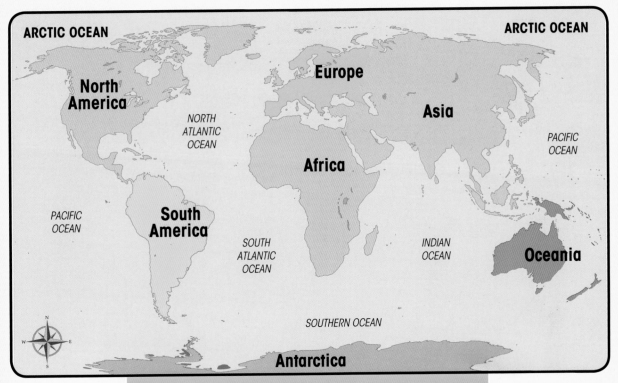

ARCTIC OCEAN

ARCTIC OCEAN

North America

Europe

Asia

NORTH ATLANTIC OCEAN

PACIFIC OCEAN

Africa

PACIFIC OCEAN

South America

SOUTH ATLANTIC OCEAN

INDIAN OCEAN

Oceania

SOUTHERN OCEAN

N
W E
S

Antarctica

The Arctic Ocean is at the top of the world and is roughly circular in shape.

The five oceans are joined and water flows between them. The oceans are mostly divided up by the seven **continents**. The Arctic Ocean is almost surrounded by the land of Europe, Asia, North America and Greenland. It is partly covered by ice all year.

The Arctic Ocean is made up of **seas**. Seas are smaller areas of an ocean found near the land. Seas are also partly surrounded by land. The Barents Sea is one of the largest seas in the Arctic Ocean.

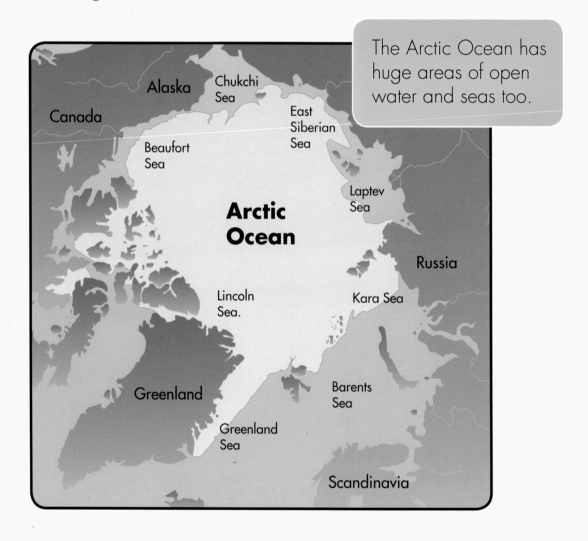

The Arctic Ocean has huge areas of open water and seas too.

Alaska

Chukchi Sea

Canada

East Siberian Sea

Beaufort Sea

Laptev Sea

Arctic Ocean

Russia

Lincoln Sea.

Kara Sea

Greenland

Barents Sea

Greenland Sea

Scandinavia

Icebreaker ships are needed to travel through the Bering Strait.

Bering Sea

Bethel

Anadyr

Providerniya

Bering Strait

Nome

Alaska (United States)

Pevek

Cherskij

Chukchi Sea

Ostrov Vrangely

East Siberian Sea

Barrow

Prudhoe Bay

Beaufort Sea

A **strait** is a narrow corridor of water that links seas and oceans. The Bering Strait lies between Alaska and Russia. It links the Arctic Ocean with the Bering Sea and separates the **continents** of Asia and North America at their closest point.

Geography

Large parts of the Arctic Ocean are very shallow. That is because there are very wide and shallow **continental shelves** below the water. A continental shelf is the land at the edge of a **continent** that lies under the ocean.

The ocean water looks lighter where the continental shelf is shallower.

Arctic Ocean fact file

Total area of ocean:	About 14 million square kilometres (about 5.4 million square miles)
Average depth:	987 metres (3,240 feet)
Length of coastline:	45,390 kilometres (28,200 miles)
Deepest point:	Litke Deep in the Eurasian Basin 5,450 metres (17,880 feet)

There are some deeper areas on the ocean floor called basins. There are also four huge **mountain ranges** called ridges that rise up from the Arctic Ocean floor. These are the Alpha Ridge, Gakkel Ridge, Lomonosov Ridge and Mendeleev Ridge, an extension of the Alpha Ridge.

Weather

Winters at the Arctic Ocean are very cold. In most places the temperature is −30°C to −35°C (−22°F to −31°F) and in others it is even colder. There are few clouds and it hardly ever rains. From October to March the sun does not appear above the **horizon**.

At certain times of the year, people fishing in the Arctic Ocean are in the dark for most of the day.

It is hard for ships to see where they are going when it is foggy over the Arctic Ocean.

In summer (June to September) it gets a bit warmer, but it is still very cold. There is rain and snow and there is often fog over the ocean. In summer the **North Pole** has sunlight all day and all night.

Arctic ice

The centre of the Arctic Ocean is so cold that its surface stays frozen all year. Here the ice is about 3 metres (10 feet) thick. In winter, more water freezes and the surface of the Arctic Ocean is almost completely covered in ice.

In the Arctic Ocean there are huge flat blocks of floating ice called **ice floes**.

These maps show that more of the Arctic Ocean is frozen in winter (March) than by the end of summer (September).

winter   summer

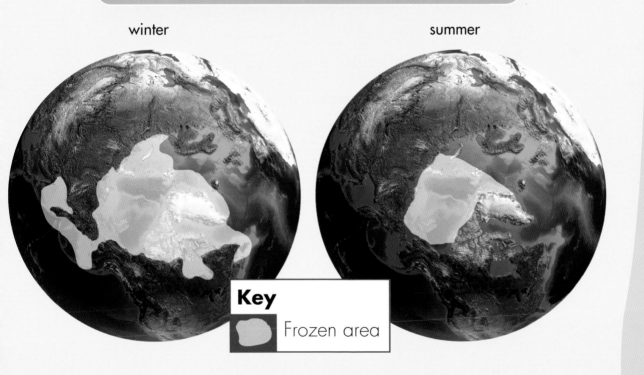

Key

Frozen area

In summer, the edges of the Arctic Ocean melt. In shallow areas of water around the **continents**, there is no ice in summer. Then the ice in the centre of the ocean is surrounded by open water.

Icebergs

Icebergs are huge chunks of ice that break off **glaciers** and fall into the Arctic Ocean. A glacier is a huge block or river of ice that moves very slowly across land.

Giant icebergs can cause big waves when they break off a glacier and fall into the ocean.

Icebergs look like huge frozen mountains floating in the Arctic Ocean.

Icebergs are huge and heavy, but they float on the ocean. Only the top part of an iceberg shows above the water. You cannot see the biggest part of an iceberg because it is under the water.

Islands

The Arctic **Archipelago** is a group of 36,563 islands that lie north of Canada. Most of these islands are small, but 94 are large. Baffin, Victoria, Ellesmere, Banks and Prince of Wales are large islands.

An island is an area of land surrounded by water. Many Arctic islands are small and uninhabited.

The Lofoten islands are unusually mild. The land does not freeze, so people live here all year round.

The land on most of the Arctic islands is frozen for much of the year. Most islands are uninhabited, which means no one lives on them. Some islands are flat. Some have high mountains covered in ice.

Resources

Oil and gas are valuable resources found under the Arctic Ocean. People collect these fuels from under the ocean floor. In some parts of the Arctic Ocean there are oil platforms above the water which people use to drill for oil under the ocean floor.

This huge oil platform is in the Beaufort Sea, in the Arctic Ocean.

If ships are damaged they could spill the oil they carry into the Arctic Ocean.

Ships carry some of the oil and gas across the ocean. Some people worry that the oil could spill into the Arctic. It is very hard to clean up spilled oil in the Arctic because it is so cold, dangerous and remote. Oil spills would harm many animals and the places where they live.

Ports

Ships load and unload goods at **ports** on coasts around the Arctic Ocean. A port is a place at the edge of an ocean where ships stop. The Port of Churchill is Canada's only active Arctic seaport. Huge ships take wheat from Canada to sell in Europe and other places.

Ships can only stop at Churchill between July and November because the port is covered in ice for the rest of the year.

Large amounts of coal, oil, metals and other types of cargo are also shipped out of Murmansk.

The port of Murmansk in northwestern Russia is a busy fishing port on the Barents Sea. The water here does not completely ice over so ships can use this port all year round.

People

Inuit people have lived along the Arctic coast of Canada, Greenland, Alaska and Russia for 4,000 years. In the past, they lived in igloos made from ice or tents made from animal skins. They caught fish from kayaks made from wood or bones covered in skins.

Today, most Inuit people live in towns and cities and some work in mines and oil fields.

Scientists use special equipment to study the weather, water and wildlife in the Arctic region.

Scientists come to study in the Arctic. They live and work in research stations. Some research stations are on islands or on the coasts of the **continents**. Some research stations rest on giant floating slabs of ice!

Animals

Polar bears are famous Arctic animals.
They have thick fur and a thick layer of fat called
blubber to keep them warm. They use their huge
paws to paddle through the ocean to **ice floes**.
They catch seals resting on ice floes or that come
up to breathe through holes in ice floes.

Polar bears have blubber
that is 11 centimetres
(4 inches) thick to stop
them freezing in the
Arctic Ocean.

Walruses use their huge tusks to fight and pull themselves onto the ice!

Walruses and bowhead whales also have a thick layer of blubber to keep them warm. The bowhead's blubber may be 60 centimetres (24 inches) thick! Walruses use their **flippers** for crawling and swimming. They swim to find animals to eat, such as clams, on the ocean floor.

Famous places

The **North Pole** is the northernmost point on Earth. It lies in the middle of the Arctic Ocean. The first explorers who proved they reached the North Pole got here in 1926. The first ship to visit the North Pole was a submarine in 1958. It came up through the ice!

Modern explorers still take the challenge of reaching the North Pole.

Tysfjorden is the second deepest fjord in Norway, with a maximum depth of about 900 metres (3,000 feet).

The amazing fjords along the coast of the Arctic Ocean in Norway are world-famous. A fjord is a long, narrow, deep body of water between high cliffs. Sogn Fjord is the longest and deepest fjord in Norway. It measures 1,308 metres (4,291 feet) at its deepest point.

Fun facts

- The temperature at much of the surface of the Arctic Ocean is −2°C (28°F), which is when salty seawater freezes.

- Over recent years, the area of Arctic ice has shrunk because more of it is melting. Many scientists believe this is because of global warming. They believe Earth's temperatures are rising because people are changing the Earth's atmosphere by burning up lots of fuel.

- The Arctic Ocean is about one and a half times as big as the USA.

- Polar bears only live in the Arctic, not the Antarctic.

- The Arctic Ocean is less than a tenth of the size of the Pacific Ocean.

Quiz

1 Where is the **North Pole**?

2 Which is the smallest ocean in the world?

3 What are icebergs?

4 How do polar bears keep warm in the Arctic?

Answers

1 The North Pole is in the centre of the Arctic Ocean.

2 The Arctic is the smallest ocean in the world.

3 Icebergs are giant blocks of floating ice.

4 Polar bears have thick hair and a thick layer of fat called **blubber** to keep them warm.

Glossary

archipelago group or row of islands close together

blubber thick layer of fat under an animal's skin

continent one of seven huge areas of land on Earth

continental shelf (more than one are called **continental shelves**) part of a continent that is underwater

flipper flat part on the sides of an animal's body that is usually used for swimming

glacier huge block or river of ice that moves very slowly across land

horizon line where the sky seems to meet the land or the ocean

ice floes huge flat blocks of ice floating at the surface of an ocean

Inuit first group of people who lived in the Arctic

mountain range group or chain of mountains that are close together

North Pole northernmost point on Earth

port place at the edge of an ocean where ships stop

sea smaller area of an ocean usually found near the land and usually partly surrounded by land

strait narrow corridor of water linking a sea and ocean

Find out more

Books

Arctic and Antarctic (Eyewitness), Barbara Taylor
  (Dorling Kindersley, 2012)

Expedition to the Arctic (Travelling Wild), Alex Woolf
  (Wayland, 2012)

The Open Ocean (Watery Worlds), Jinny Johnson
  (Franklin Watts, 2012)

Websites

Learn more about the Arctic Ocean and its wildlife at
www.bbc.co.uk/oceans/locations/arctic

This website is about the ways people are trying to
protect the Arctic
www.oceanconservancy.org/places/arctic

Index